NEWTON & GRAVITY

Paul Strathern was born in London and studied philosophy at Trinity College, Dublin. He was a lecturer at Kingston University where he taught philosophy and mathematics. He is a Somerset Maugham prize-winning novelist. He is also the author of the *Philosophers in 90 Minutes* series. He wrote *Mendeleyev's Dream* which was shortlisted for the Aventis Science Book Prize, *Dr. Strangelove's Game: A History of Economic Genius*, *The Medici: Godfathers of the Renaissance*, *Napoleon in Egypt* and most recently, *The Artist, The Philosopher and The Warrior*, which details the convergence of three of Renaissance Italy's most brilliant minds: Leonardo Da Vinci, Niccolo Machiavelli and Cesare Borgia. He lives in London and has three grandchildren.

In THE BIG IDEA series:

NEWTON & GRAVITY
The Big Idea
PAUL STRATHERN

arrow books

Reissued by Arrow Books 2010

1 3 5 7 9 10 8 6 4 2

Copyright © Paul Strathern, 1997

Paul Strathern has asserted his right under the Copyright,
Designs and Patents Act, 1988, to be identified as
the author of this work.

This book is sold subject to the condition that it shall not,
by way of trade or otherwise, be lent, resold, hired out, or
otherwise circulated without the publisher's prior consent in
any form of binding or cover other than that in which it is
published and without a similar condition including this
condition being imposed on the
subsequent purchaser.

First published in Great Britain in 1997 by Arrow Books

The Random House Group Limited
20 Vauxhall Bridge Road, London, SW1V 2SA

www.rbooks.co.uk

Addresses for companies within The Random House Group
Limited can be found at:
www.randomhouse.co.uk/offices.htm

The Random House Group Limited Reg. No. 954009

A CIP catalogue record for this book
is available from the British Library

ISBN 9780099237624

The Random House Group Limited supports The Forest
Stewardship Council (FSC), the leading international forest
certification organisation. All our titles that are printed on
Greenpeace approved FSC certified paper carry the FSC
logo. Our paper procurement policy can be found at:
www.rbooks.co.uk/environment

Typeset by SX Composing DTP, Rayleigh, Essex

Printed and bound in Great Britain by
CPI Cox & Wyman, Reading, RG1 8EX

CONTENTS

INTRODUCTION

A good case can be made for Newton being the finest mind humanity has yet produced. Shakespeare used language as no other, Napoleon used personality as no other – but no one has ever extended the limits of human understanding quite so drastically as Newton.

His work represents an evolutionary advance in our thinking – one giant leap for mankind. Long before we landed on the moon (or even considered doing so) Newton's mathematics paved the way for such a feat. Before Newton, the moon was part of the heavens, subject to unknown heavenly laws of its own. After him it became a satellite of earth, kept in orbit by the planet's gravitational pull. Humanity had its first glimpse of how the entire universe worked.

But the discovery of universal gravity was only

the most major of Newton's many major discoveries. The concept of force, calculus, the nature of light, the theory of mechanics, the binomial series, Newton's method in numerical analysis – the list goes on and on. More units, and scientific and mathematical entities, are named after Newton than after any other scientist. The newton (the SI, or internationally agreed, unit of force), Newtonian fluid, Newton's formula (for lenses), Newton's rings (in optics), the Newton quotient (in differentiation) and many more – each the direct result of his work.

Yet all this was only possible because Newton arrived at the right moment in history. Just as Dante could only have written his *Divine Comedy* within the rigid all-embracing hierarchy of the Middle Ages, so Newton could only have made his discoveries after Copernicus and Galileo had freed the scientific mind from those same rigidities. As Newton himself confessed: 'If I have seen a little farther than others it is because I have stood on the shoulders of giants'.

The chains of medieval restraint had fallen away, and the door of human knowledge had opened upon a new world. In Newton's view, he had achieved little: 'I seem to have been only like a boy playing on the seashore, and diverting myself in now and then finding a smoother pebble or a prettier shell than ordinary, whilst the great ocean of truth lay all undiscovered before me'. The modesty exhibited here is of course dwarfed by the oceanic vision – which he alone was in a position to see. An implication that Newton may well have intended. He was not by nature modest.

So what kind of man was the possessor of the greatest intellect in history? In general, Newton's contemporaries came to regard him much as we in the 20th century regarded Einstein. A tame eccentric, member of a rare protected species, the absent-minded genius of unquestionable moral stature: a distant but faintly loveable figure – vouchsafed enormous gravitas by the sheer weight of his achievements. In his time, Newton was the solitary scholar chosen by his peers as MP for Cambridge University, the revered president of the Royal Society re-elected unopposed year after year, the Master of the Royal Mint feared and hated by the counterfeiters of the London underworld. As is so often the case, it was the common people who recognised the man for what he was. For beneath the austere public façade lay a deeply disturbed and vindictive personality, harbouring his own illicit secrets.

LIFE AND WORKS

Isaac Newton was born on Christmas day 1642, in the manor house at the hamlet of Woolsthorpe in Lincolnshire. By coincidence his great scientific predecessor Galileo had died earlier in the same year.

Nowhere in the Newton family tree is there any sign of exceptional predecessors. His father, also Isaac Newton, was a prospering yeoman who could not even sign his name. 'A wild, extravagant, weak man,' according to his family, he died three months before the birth of his son. His mother was the daughter of an impecunious local gentleman, and was generally regarded as a hard-working, frugal woman.

Isaac was born prematurely, and was 'so little they could fit him into a quart pot'. He was not expected to survive the day of his birth. (In the event, he was to have exceptional health and live for 84 years.) Having never known his father, young Isaac was to 'lose' his mother when he was just 18 months old. In 1644 Hannah Newton married the 63-year-old Barnabas Smith, a well-off local minister, and went to live in the village of North Witham. Young Isaac was left behind, to be looked after by his grandmother.

Newton never forgot this traumatic event, and its effect left an indelible imprint on his character. His adult life was to be marred by uncontrollable rages, paranoid vindictiveness and occasional mental instability. He loved his mother, but she had abandoned him. He couldn't bring himself to hate her, but heaven help anyone who presented a legitimate target on which he could vent his repressed inner fury.

In fact, North Witham was only a couple of miles up the valley. Young Isaac could even see its church tower across the fields from the hill above his home. But in reality it remained a world away. His true father was 'in heaven', and his mother withdrawn to the limits of his childhood world. In adult life Newton was to devote himself to long and profound speculation about distant heavenly bodies and the nature of their attraction to one another. Not surprisingly, psychologists have seen more than unalloyed coincidence at work here.

According to a contemporary, Newton grew up a 'sober, silent, thinking lad'. But he was also subject to occasional outbursts of 'tantrums'. During one of these Newton was later to remember 'threatening my father and mother Smith to burn them and the house over them'. So it seems that initially his mother wasn't always spared his wrath. (And pyromania, even in wishful form, hardly betokens normality.)

But Newton's mind wasn't the only thing on fire. In the year of his birth the behaviour of Charles I and his belief in 'the divine right of kings' finally drove the Parliamentarians to challenge his rule. The ensuing Civil War raged all over England during the first six years of Newton's life, ending in victory for the Parliamentarians and the execution of Charles I in 1649. Throughout the Civil War sporadic fighting and house-burning took place in Lincolnshire. Newton and other local landowning families were inclined to support the king, but not to the extent of taking up arms.

The Parliamentary victory – the first successful revolution in Europe – saw the establishment of the Commonwealth, followed by post-revolutionary excesses such as have now become the norm. A repressive Puritanism was enforced. All dancing and displays of public merriment were banned, and even Christmas became a day of prayer rather than pudding-eating. Yet here again the farming families of Lincolnshire were hardly affected. They had long lived austere God-fearing lives, with the emphasis on bible reading and the shockingness of sex. Young Isaac grew up in a habitually puritan household, and absorbed puritan habits as a matter of course. He learned to consult the Bible to discover the wishes of God the father, a habit he was to retain throughout his life.

But God the father was not only God in heaven, he was also father in heaven. In the ever-booming field of Newtonian psychological studies, most are agreed that Newton was driven by a strong unconscious need to know his father. He knew from his faith that God the father had made the universe, leaving certain clues as to its ultimate nature and His ultimate intentions.

Throughout his life Newton was driven to search obsessively for these clues — in the two appropriate fields. He was to devote just as much of his time to pursuing biblical and religious studies, as he was to the pursuit of scientific truth. And to the end, he was convinced that his religious work would have the most lasting value. For once, the facts appear to be as mad as the psychology.

When Newton was 10, the Reverend Barnabas Smith died and Isaac's mother returned home to Woolsthorpe a comparatively rich woman. Newton's prayers had been answered. There followed two years of curious bliss, tempered by the common-sense reality of his mother, and the additional presence of a half-brother and two half-sisters. But Isaac was the oldest, and Hannah seems to a certain extent to have relied upon him. Before Isaac had even reached puberty he had become 'the man of the family' in his mother's eyes. The basic self-belief engendered by this precocious motherly recognition was never to desert him in his intellectual endeavours, even when the man himself was beset by maddening anxieties.

At the age of 12, Newton went to the

grammar school in Grantham, which was 10 miles away. Here he took lodgings with Mr Clark the apothecary, whose house was on the High Street beside the George Inn. At school his studies consisted almost entirely of latin and ancient greek. Mathematics was all but ignored in the education of the period, which remained for the most part medieval. The quiet, sensitive country boy was uninterested, and sank to the bottom of the class.

According to his own account, Newton remained intellectually dormant until the day when he was kicked in the stomach by the school bully. Newton challenged him to a fight in the church yard. In the words of Newton's first biographer Conduitt, who recorded Newton's reminiscences: 'Isaac was not so lusty as his antagonist [but] he had so much more spirit and resolution that he beat him till he declared he would fight no more'. Newton had found a legitimate target on which to vent the dreadful anger that lay repressed within him. But once this was aroused it became uncontrollable, and then there was no holding him back. Trouncing his physically superior opponent was not enough. After his victory 'Isaac pulled him along by the ears and thrust his face against the side of the church and rub his nose against the wall'. But even such physical humiliation was not sufficient. Newton had to defeat his opponent in every way possible. He felt the need to better his opponent intellectually, began trying in class, and was soon demonstrating his intellectual superiority.

This is the way Newton remembered it, and there is no doubt that something very similar happened. Such anger-fuelled vindictiveness was to recur at intervals throughout his life: this outbreak merely set the pattern.

Once Newton's intellectual faculties had been roused, there was no stopping him. Watching the teenage dullard emerge from his chrysalis and stretch the butterfly wings of genius must have been a wondrous sight for the townsfolk of Grantham. And of course they all remembered it. In hindsight. According to reminiscences collected after the death of the great Sir Isaac Newton, President of the Royal Society, Master of The Royal Mint etc, young Isaac displayed all the expected signs of supreme genius – baffling the locals with intricately constructed model windmills, hand-made water clocks, exploding kites, a mouse-driven corn mill, a foldable paper lantern, his ability to tell the precise time from a shadow, and a notebook filled with the usual unintelligible diagrams. Fortunately this notebook is now in the Pierpont Morgan Library in New York, an inscription inside the front cover recording that it was originally bought by Newton for 2½d (old pennies) in 1659. Its contents confirm the seemingly fanciful memories of the people of Grantham, with pages containing diagrams of Copernicus' solar system, details of how to make a sundial and construct a model windmill, and astronomical predictions of eclipses. Two things are obvious. Newton's intellectual interests had expanded far beyond the limits of his school education. And his main interest was in science and how things worked.

All the evidence points to a precociously brilliant, largely self-taught amateur. Unusual, but not unique. There must have been a score or more of similar prodigies throughout the land. Like the great majority of the others, Newton seemed destined to eccentric provincial mediocrity. In the same year as he bought his tu'penny ha'penny notebook, his mother called him home to run the farm. He was just 17.

But this time all was not sweetness and light at home. Newton's mind was now afire with something more absorbing than fantasies of pyromania (though it may well have appeared equally disturbed). Psychological explanations of Newton's sudden all-consuming obsession with science abound – from discovering Father's clues, to a demented need for escape into an ordered world free from psychic anxiety. (This complex and often contradictory multiplicity of explanations is useful, if only as a reminder of the complex and often contradictory nature of the unique entity it attempts to describe: Newton's mind.) But one thing is certain, this overwhelming interest in science gripped Newton's adolescent mind with the force of an addiction. (And was to retain such force, virtually without ceasing, for *37 years*.)

As a farmer the 17-year-old Newton was worse than useless. Set to watch over the sheep, he would settle in the shade of a tree with a book. When he went to market in Grantham, he left the farmhand to sell the produce and livestock while he nipped round to the house of his former landlord Mr Clark to pick up some more books (one of Mr Clark's relatives had left his collection in the attic). The sheep broke loose over the hills, the pigs overran the neighbour's cornfields, and the boundary fences fell into an illegal state of disrepair. As a result Newton was hauled before the courts and fined four shillings and four pennies. (The cost of a good pair of shoes.) Newton's first official qualification was a criminal record.

Mother had no idea what to do, and life at home was fraught. In a 'list of sins' which Newton drew up some years later, this period includes such items as: 'Peevishness with my mother', 'Falling out with the servants', 'Refusing to go to the close at my mother's command', and 'Punching my sister'. Like most teenagers, he knew what he didn't want to do. Unlike most teenagers, he knew precisely what he did want to do. Newton continued reading avidly, making models, conducting scientific experiments, calculating and sketching diagrams in his notebook.

Fortunately two people had recognised Newton's exceptional talents. One was John

Stokes, his schoolmaster at Grantham; the other was his maternal uncle William Ayscough, rector of the nearby village of Burton Coggles, who happened to be a graduate of Trinity College, Cambridge. Between them, they managed to persuade Newton's mother to send him back to school in Grantham, where Stokes could prepare him for entrance to Trinity College, Cambridge.

Newton returned to live with Mr Clark the apothecary, where he continued to devour the collection of books, and now began decorating his room with all kinds of drawings. According to Mr Clark's stepdaughter, he also formed a romantic attachment with her during this period. She was several years younger than him, and the romance appears to have been largely of her own imagining. This is the only occasion in Newton's life when his name was to be romantically linked with a woman.

Newton went up to Cambridge in June 1661, where he was admitted to Trinity College. According to a contemporary historian, Trinity College was at the time 'the stateliest and most uniform College in Christendom'. Its academic prowess was entering a similar class to its

appearance – though Cambridge was still generally seen as lagging behind the great universities
of Europe, such as the Sorbonne and Padua.
England had not only undergone a political revolution, it was in the process of an intellectual one
which was unsurpassed (and as yet largely un-
recognised) in Europe. This was to culminate in
the works of Newton – but its lesser lights
included men of such stature as Harvey (whose
discovery of the circulation of the blood ushered
in modern medicine), Halley (the great
astronomer, after whom the comet is named),
Hobbes (the most perceptive political theorist of
his era), Locke (whose Empiricism changed the
course of philosophy, and whose social ideas
were to shape the US constitution), and Boyle
(the pioneer chemist).

Newton was 18 when he arrived at
Cambridge, two years older than the average
student. He was also much poorer than the average student, and was only admitted as a sizar. This
required him to act as a form of valet to his tutor.
Fortunately, his tutor only deigned to take up
residence for five weeks of the year, so Newton
had most of his time to himself.

There were few distractions at Cambridge in those days. According to a visiting German traveller, outside the university itself Cambridge was 'no better than a village . . . one of the sorriest places in the world'. The village taverns were filled with jolly trollopes and roistering young gentlefolk. (These were Newton's fellow undergraduates, less than a third of whom bothered to take a degree.) The year prior to Newton's arrival Charles II had ascended to the throne. After the puritan excesses of the Commonwealth, the more conspicuous excesses of the Restoration era were now in full swing. But Newton's puritanism did not depend upon the political climate. Between marathon bouts of studying, which frequently lasted until dawn, Newton might sit in his rooms making lists of his sins (none of which ever rose to roistering or trollopes).

Despite the growing intellectual revolution in England, education in the universities remained for the most part heavily rooted in the Aristotelianism of the medieval era. The earth still stood at the centre of the universe, which consisted of earth, air, fire and water. These 'elements' were reflected in our four 'humours': blood, phlegm, choler and melancholy, whose 'balance' governed our health. And so forth . . . An invincibly coherent world according to its own assumptions, whose inadequacy was only gradually exposed.

The first serious cracks in the edifice of Aristotelianism had begun to appear in Europe during the early 17th century. The Polish priest Copernicus had suggested a heliocentric solar system. This had led the German astronomer Kepler, working in Prague, to propose laws of planetary motion. The Italian physicist Galileo had then put forward a new mechanics based on this (before being forced to recant his views by the Catholic Church). Meanwhile Descartes' philosophy of doubt had shown Aristotelianism, the basis of the Church's scientific teaching, to be devoid of analytic or perceptual justification. Such were the pioneers who stimulated the English intellectual revolution, and the undergraduate Newton was soon becoming heavily influenced by their discoveries.

Of equal importance, Newton also began learning the new mathematics which supported these discoveries, and upon which any future discoveries would need to be based. During the previous century the advances in astronomy and navigation had required new and more refined methods of calculation and exactitude. As a result mathematics had undergone a revolution which paralleled the recent scientific discoveries. Here too the lineaments of an increasingly precise structure were beginning to emerge from the medieval mists. In 1585 the Flemish civil servant Stevin proposed the decimal system for measurement of amounts less than one; and in the early years of the 17th century the Scottish baron Napier invented logarithms. This mathematical revolution had come to full flower in France. Here three of the greatest mathematicians of all time – Descartes, Fermat and Pascal – had all reached the height of their powers by the mid 17th century.

During Newton's undergraduate period he studied and absorbed the lessons of Descartes (though how much he knew of Pascal and Fermat remains an open question). Descartes had invented Cartesian co-ordinates (named after him): the three axes which enabled every geometric point (or straight line, or curve, or shape) in space to be precisely mapped. Algebra was also introduced into geometry, liberating it from the particularity of arithmetic, and analytic geometry was born. A curve could now be represented by an equation, as in the two-axis figure below.

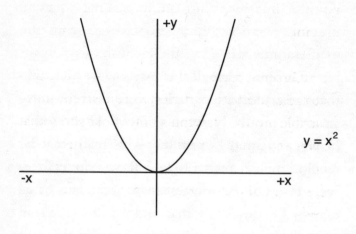

More significantly, Descartes' mathematics (and his philosophy) viewed the world as a vast intricate mechanical apparatus. Previously, Aristotelianism had viewed the world in terms of qualities (earth, air etc), now it was viewed in terms of quantities – which could be measured.

Newton began keeping a notebook, entitled 'Certain Philosophical questions', (*Quaestiones quaedam Philosophcae*) with a heading: 'My best friend is truth'. In this we see him absorbing Descartes' proposal that all reality consists of particles of matter in motion, and that all natural phenomena come about through the interaction of these particles. The French scientist-philosopher Gassendi revived the ancient Greek notion that these ultimate particles were discrete indestructible atoms. Newton's notebooks show that he was also aware of parallel developments by the Anglo-Irish chemist Boyle, whose experiments were beginning to suggest the existence of basic chemical elements.

Boyle's discoveries laid the groundwork for Newton's future work in chemistry, but Newton's interest in chemistry was hardly forward-looking. In the 17th century chemistry was only just beginning to emerge from the mumbo-jumbo of alchemy. In pursuit of his chemical interests, Newton also began reading works on alchemy, magic and the hermetic tradition.

These purported to explain natural phenomena in terms of metaphysical gobbledegook.

It would be nice to think that Newton read all this nonsense by way of light amusement, after the extremely exacting rigors of his mathematical and scientific studies. But this was not the case. Newton took his alchemy seriously. This was on a par with his obsessive study of the Bible. Here too, he might find clues as to Father's identity.

These two ways of looking at the world – the physical and the metaphysical – would seem to us mere mortals to be mutually exclusive. But they were not for Newton. Indeed, the contradictions between these two world views appears to have acted in some ways as a stimulant to his mental processes.

But Newton's discoveries were not all fool's gold. By the time he had been an undergraduate for three years, Newton was already making important mathematical discoveries. He had worked out the Binomial Theorem for fractions. The Binomial Theorem involves the formula for the expansion of a binomial expression. That is, one containing the sum of two variables, such as

$(x + y)$, raised to a given power n – expressed $(x + y)^n$.

A simple example shows:

$$(x + y)^2 = x^2 + 2xy + y^2$$

But when n (the power) is not a whole number, the expansion becomes an infinite series.

An example with a single variable is as follows:

$$(1 + x)^{1/2} = 1 + \tfrac{1}{2}x - \tfrac{1}{8}x^2 + \tfrac{1}{16}x^3 + \ldots$$

and so on ad infinitum.

Newton worked out a general rule for such expansions. As we shall see, this work on infinite series was Newton's first step towards one of the greatest mathematical discoveries of all time: calculus.

Newton received his BA in June 1665. Professor Barrow, his examiner, formed 'an indifferent opinion' of his abilities: Newton didn't even know his basic Euclid. Newton had indeed sorely neglected the syllabus. What Professor Barrow didn't realise was that Newton was already advancing beyond Descartes, who in his turn had already advanced beyond Euclid. Newton was almost entirely self-taught – in the sense that he worked largely alone, from books. All his truly amazing work was confined to his notebooks – which nobody else had seen. Despite the gaps in his knowledge, Newton was allowed to continue studying for an MA. (Students who actually studied were evidently a rarity in need of preservation.)

Newton seemed to thrive in isolation, and events now conspired to make sure this continued. Late in 1664 two French sailors had been found in the London slums around Drury Lane dying of the bubonic plague. The disease quickly spread throughout the city (it was eventually to cause over 80,000 deaths in London alone), and then out along the stagecoach routes and cattle drovers' trails into the country at large. All who could began to flee the centres of population, and by August 1665 Cambridge University had effectively closed down. Newton returned to Woolsthorpe, where he remained for around a year.

This was to result in an *annus mirabilis* the like of which has never been seen in science before or since. (The only near competitor was Einstein's

1905, when he discovered the Special Theory of Relativity, proposed that light consisted of quanta, and provided the molecular explanation of Brownian Movement.)

Newton's first major breakthrough was the development of calculus. The ability to represent an algebraic formula on a graph now meant that certain algebraic problems were susceptible to geometric solutions. For instance, the rate of change of x against y for any given values (ie, at any given point on a curve) is the tangent to the curve at that point.

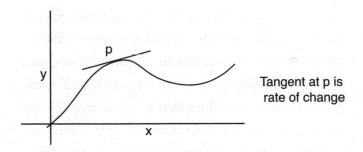

Tangent at p is rate of change

It's easy enough to find the tangent to a circle, or even a regular curve, but how do we find it for a variable curve? This is done by calculus. The basic notion of calculus was discovered by the ancient Greeks.

In order to determine the area of a circle, Archimedes inscribed within it an equilateral polygon, whose area he knew how to calculate. If he increased the number of sides, the area of the polygon increased, approaching the area of the circle – which was its upper limit. (Similarly, by enclosing the circle in an equilateral polygon, he could approach the lower limit: the answer lying between these two sums.)

However, if the sides of either polygon were increased to infinite this also would give the area of the circle.

This principle could similarly be applied to the tangent to a curve.

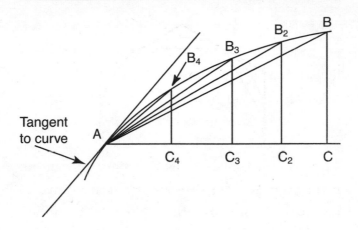

As the distance between A and B becomes infinitely small, tending towards its limit zero, the side AB opposite the right angle ACB approximates closer to the tangent, becoming this at the limit.

The same principle can be applied in calculating the area beneath a curve.

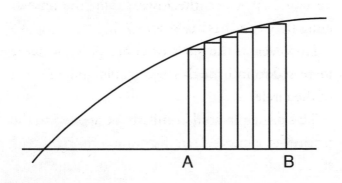

As the number of rectangles between A and B is increased towards infinite, their area approaches the area under the curve as their limit.

Once again, this was a problem with an infinite series arising from functions with two variables – just as Newton had dealt with in Binomial Theorem. To begin with, the calculations involved in such problems were seen as involving static sums of infinitely small quantities. Newton's great insight was to see this problem instead as one of *mobility* – treating the curve not as a static object, but as the locus of a *moving point*. (Indicatively Newton first called his method 'fluxions', implying flow – not calculus, as it was later to be known.) His innovation was thus to introduce the notion of time.

Newton's method for finding the tangent to a point on a curve is now known as differential calculus. This regards the ever-varying quantity of a *moving point* as if it was made up of an infinitely large number of infinitely tiny changes.

For instance, the velocity (v) of a body at a particular instant is seen as the infinitessimally small distance it covers (ds) in the infinitessimally small, decreasing to zero, amount of time (dt).

Therefore

$$v = \frac{ds}{dt}$$

Now as dt $\rightarrow$ 0 (ie, reaches its limit at zero) so v reaches the limit which is its exact speed at the given moment.

Fortunately Newton's long and mind-bogglingly complex calculations eventually yielded an easily applicable rule of thumb – as used by all budding mathematicians who know what to do, but don't really know what they're doing. ('Just follow the rule, young man.') Put in the very simplest terms, for the formula:

$$y = x^n$$

the derivative $\frac{dy}{dx} = n\,x^{n-1}$

For example: make n = 2. Thus the formula becomes:

$$y = x^2$$

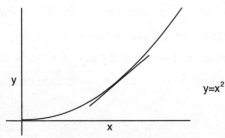

$$y=x^2$$

The rate of change at *any* point, $\dfrac{dx}{dy}$, equals $2x^{2-1}$

$$= 2x$$

In other words, the gradient of the tangent at any point on the curve will always be 2x.

This process of differential calculus provided the new mathematics with one of its most powerful tools – allowing the calculation of all kinds of rates of change. This included for instance the maximum and minimum points in any curve – which occur when the gradient, or the rate of change, $\dfrac{dx}{dy}$, is equal to zero:

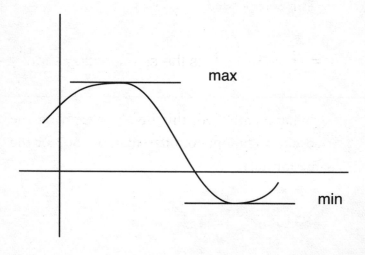

Newton then went on to extend his method of fluxions to include what is now known as integral calculus. This is essentially the reverse technique to differential calculus, and is used for calculating the area beneath a curve.

For example, the velocity of a point (v) can be expressed in terms of the infinitely small distance ds travelled in the brief moment dt. Thus

$$ds = v\, dt$$

The measurable distance s which the point travels between time t_1 and t_2 is found by continuously summing the changes in this interval, which is known as integration.

This is expressed:

$$s = \int_{t_2}^{t_1} v\, dt \qquad \left(\int \text{ is the sign for integration} \right)$$

Greatly simplified, this involves applying the opposite technique to differentiation. So, for the same formula

$$y = x^n$$

instead of $\dfrac{dy}{dx} = n\, x^{n-1}$

for integration we get $\displaystyle\int_{t_2}^{t_1} x^n \, dx = \frac{x^{n+1}}{n+1}$

This immensely useful technique could be used for such problems as finding the area of any kind of shape described by a formulaic curve (and rotating about the axis produced a volume). It could also be used for any problem where continuous summing of infinitessimal changes was required.

At this stage, Newton's calculus still remained in embryo form. But even so, he now had the technique which enabled him to undertake his major work. Newton's transcendent achievement during the course of 1665-6 was of course concerning gravity.

Newton was later asked how he had achieved this and his other epoch-making discoveries. 'By always thinking unto them,' he replied. 'I keep the subject constantly before me and wait until the first dawnings open little by little into the full light.' According to the famous story, the 'first dawnings' of his theory of gravity came to Newton when he saw an apple drop from a tree. This is often dismissed as sheer legend. But according to Newton's early biographer Stukely: 'he told me . . . the notion of gravitation came into his mind . . . occasion'd by the fall of an apple, as he sat in contemplative mood'.

It is important to understand the full significance of what Newton understood at that moment. What did he know already, and what did his eventual theory of gravity explain?

The key to it all was Kepler – who had taken over 20 years of painstaking observation and endless calculation before arriving at his three laws of planetary motion. These were published in 1609 and stated: 1, the planets travel in ellipses around the sun, and the sun is at one focus of these eliptical orbits; 2, a straight line joining the sun and a planet sweeps out equal areas in equal times; (in the diagram below: time taken for planet p to travel from a to b, is the same as from c to d, and the area x is equal to area y); 3, the square of the time taken for one complete orbit by a planet, is proportional to the cube of its average distance from the sun; (in the diagram: if planet p takes time T to complete an orbit, and r is the average radius of this orbit, then: $T^2 = r^3$).

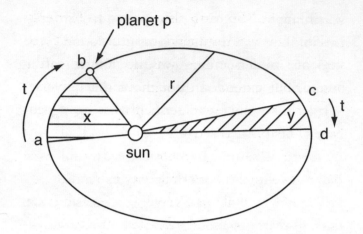

T = time taken to complete one orbit

Meanwhile back on earth, Galileo had confirmed by experiments, said to have been conducted from the Leaning Tower of Pisa, that a falling body accelerates at a uniform rate. He also derived a formula for the parabolic path of a projectile – such as the path of a stone thrown over a distance, or a ball fired from a cannon.

Newton's genius was to put Kepler's laws and Galileo's findings together. The notion of gravity which came to him when the apple fell from the tree would eventually be seen as the same power which held the moon in orbit around the earth, and the planets in orbit around the sun. The laws which applied on earth also applied to heavenly bodies. This was a stupendous intuition. At one step our understanding was no longer earth-bound, but extended throughout the universe. (Kepler's laws merely described what happened, Newton explained *why*.)

Newton was not to publish his ideas for over 20 years. There are several reasons for this. At first he only regarded gravity as applying on earth. Later, when he extended this to extra-terrestrial bodies, he couldn't quite work out the mathematics of it. How did the earth's gravitational force actually work? Did it attract the moon from its centre or from its surface, or from somewhere in between? Not until he had refined the techniques of his newly discovered calculus was he able to overcome such problems. Yet these weren't the only reason for his silence.

Some have called Newton a secretive character. But this is not strictly true. The fact is, Newton couldn't abide being contradicted, even in the most trivial matter. It was liable to make him burst into one of his uncontrollable rages. So rather than face the questioning of his fellow scientists, he preferred to keep his discoveries to himself.

Needless to say, such psychology only accounts for Newton's personality. It may be likened to a map of the world. This outlines the contours and shapes, but in no way explains the magnificence and profusion of the reality. The sheer quality of Newton's mind remains utterly inexplicable.

During the 20 years before Newton published his findings on gravity, his initial insight became refined into a comprehensive system. It was this which finally appeared in his masterpiece the *Principia*. Here Newton went one step further than Kepler and Galileo, putting forward three laws of his own which superseded their findings.

Newton's first law of motion posits a theory of inertia, stating that a body remains at rest or in uniform motion along a straight line unless it is acted upon by an outside force. Things moved through space because there was nothing to stop them after they had initially been set in motion. For the first time the movement of bodies through the heavens was *explained* – without recourse to divine juggling or locomotion by angels. (Though not until three centuries later did the Big Bang Theory explain how this initial motion had come into being.)

Newton's second law of motion states that the rate of change of momentum (mass times velocity) of a moving body is proportional to the force impressed upon it. In other words, the effect of a continuous force upon a stationary body or one in uniform motion is to make it *accelerate*. Galileo had discovered this when he dropped objects from the Leaning Tower of Pisa. The pull of gravity makes a body accelerate. The same hap-

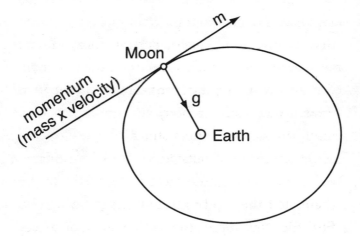

pens when the moon orbits the earth.

The continuously acting force of gravity (g) impels the moon to accelerate towards the earth, but the moon's momentum (mass x velocity) impels it along the line of force m. The resulting continuous balance of forces keeps it in orbit. To discover the force of gravity operating here, Newton had to calculate the moon's rate of change of momentum. As the moon's orbit is an irregular ellipse, this involved calculating the velocity of an object moving in a curve. It was in his earliest attempts to solve this problem that Newton employed his newly discovered flux-ions, and in the process developed differential calculus.

Newton's third law of motion states that if one body exerts a force on another, the second will exert an equal and opposite reaction on the first. Newton's concept of force in these laws was to transform science. It united Descartes' recent mechanical view of the world with the ancient tradition of Pythagoras, who claimed that the world ultimately consisted of numbers. This combining of mechanics and mathematics not only explained how the world worked, but meant we could also calculate precisely what was happening in it.

By using these three fundamental laws

Newton was finally able to conclude how gravitational force acted between two bodies. He showed that this is directly proportional to the product of their two masses, and inversely proportional to the square of the distance between their two centres. This was expressed in his cele-

$$F = \frac{m_1 \, m_2 \, G}{d^2}$$

brated formula (the $e = mc^2$ of its day):

Where F is the force of gravitational attraction, m_1 and m_2 are the masses of the earth and the moon, d is the distance between their centres, and G is the gravitational constant. What had set him on the path to this formula was the possibility of the inverse square relation – and this may well have been the original realization provoked by the falling apple. Newton didn't understand the entire notion of gravity in a flash; but this was what set him on the long and complex mathematical journey which ended in his law of gravitation. Even so, it was to be a century before the eccentric English physicist Cavendish managed to determine the value of G, the gravitational constant. However, this incompleteness didn't stop Newton from making sweeping claims for his new law. He asserted that the Law of Gravitation applied throughout the universe. This was of course a hypothesis: Newton's calculations were based entirely on observations of the moon and the discovered planets. But Newton would brook no objection, famously claiming: '*Hypotheses non fingo*'. (I do not make up hypotheses.)

It is difficult for us to understand the sheer flimsiness of Newton's claim with regard to his gravity law – which he insisted upon calling the *Universal* Law of Gravity. One of the greatest human insights of all time was in fact little more than a hunch – a guess of transcendent genius. The 20th century mathematician and philosopher Whitehead provided a useful corrective, both to Newton and us all: 'The pathetic desire of mankind to find themselves starting from an intellectual basis which is clear, distinct and certain, is illustrated by Newton's boast *hypotheses non fingo*, at the same time when he enunciated his law of universal gravitation. This law states that every particle of matter attracts every other particle of matter, though at the moment of enunciation only planets and heavenly bodies had been observed to attract "particles of matter".'

There may have been scanty *scientific* evidence for Newton's claim of universality, but it certainly accounted for many observed facts and eccentricities of planetary movement. Most interestingly, it *explained* Kepler's laws and also accounted for irregularities in the orbits of the moon and planets (these occurred when they were affected by the gravitational pull of other passing planets as well as that of the sun).

Newton's bold guess changed everything. From now on scientists believed that anything which happened in the universe could be explained in terms of mathematics. This has remained one of the central beliefs of modern science. Indeed, it is the cornerstone of the continuing quest for a Theory of Everything which will explain the fundamental workings of the universe and everything in it.

The third momentous discovery which Newton made during his *annus mirabilis* at Woolsthorpe was concerning light. Previously it had been thought that colour was created by a mixture of light and darkness. Newton realised that this was not supported by experimental evidence. The printed page of a book – which contained both white and black – did not appear coloured when viewed from a distance so that the two blended. It appeared grey.

Newton conducted a number of experiments at home in his darkened room with a glass prism. When he let in a chink of daylight between the curtains, so that a ray of white light passed through a prism, it was refracted (bent by the glass). But different parts of the beam were refracted by different amounts, and the beam emerged split into colours. These colours were the same, and in the same order, as they appeared in the rainbow: red, orange, yellow, green, blue, indigo, violet.

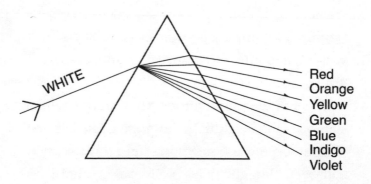

Were these colours somehow created by the clear glass of the prism? Newton now passed the rainbow beam of light through another upside down prism. The beams of coloured light then reconverged and emerged as a single beam of white light.

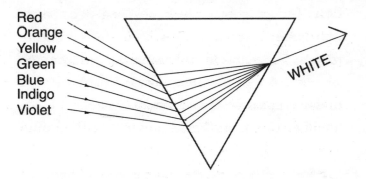

Newton then tried isolating a single beam of coloured light, and passed this through a prism. Although refracted, it emerged as the same colour. The inference was obvious. White light was made up of a combination of the colours of the spectrum.

When Newton returned to Cambridge, his demonstrations of this experiment caused quite a stir, and he was elected a fellow of Trinity College. But he remained reticent about his other discoveries. Calculus and his ideas on gravity were still in the early stages, and he had no wish to enter into discussions on these matters. (Someone might have had the temerity to contradict him.) However, he did make an exception in the case of his former tutor Barrow, the Lucasian Professor of Mathematics. (This chair had only recently been created: an early indication of Cambridge's diversification from the classical tradition and its emergence from the stranglehold of defunct Aristotelianism. The present Lucasian Professor of Mathematics is Stephen Hawking, best known as author of *A Brief History of Time*.)

Barrow was an exceptional man, in many ways the very opposite of Newton. No stereotype mathematician – he was an affable fellow of fine physique, who enjoyed boxing and had travelled as far as Constantinople (where he had won a wrestling contest). But Barrow had two points which appealed to Newton. He was a deeply religious man and a fine mathematician. Indeed, Barrow's understanding of the latest mathematical advances undoubtedly aided Newton in his development of calculus.

Unusually for a young man in his situation, Newton was not drawn towards father figures. (Father was in heaven.) A brief exception appears to have been Isaac Barrow (whose first name even echoed that of Newton's father). For once, Newton had found someone he could admire. Like Newton, Barrow worked long hours and slept little. Newton must also have recognised a similar self-absorption in Barrow's absent-mindedness, for according to one of Barrow's contemporaries he was 'most negligent in his dresse . . . like the veriest scholar that ever I mett with'. Newton presented a similar picture: 'he would go very carelessly, wth Shooes down at Heels, Stockins unty'd, surplice on, & his Head scarcely comb'd'. The professor and his 24-year-old colleague must have made a fine pair, amidst the bewigged Restoration fops.

Barrow appears to have been the only man in Cambridge who realised the truly exceptional extent of Newton's abilities. Outside the university, of course, no one had even heard of him. Yet by now Newton had made discoveries which placed him far in advance of any scientist or mathematician alive.

Barrow is said to have treated Newton as a son, giving him presents on his birthday. Though drawn to Barrow, Newton's attitude was more wary. His mother's early desertion had left him profoundly ambivalent towards the few who would manage to penetrate his carapace of other-worldly indifference.

In 1669 Barrow resigned as Lucasian Professor of Mathematics in order to pursue theological studies. He made sure that Newton was appointed in his place. The Lucasian Professor was expected to become a member of the clergy, but Barrow interceded on Newton's behalf and Newton was not required to take up holy orders. This indicates that Barrow was at least partly aware of Newton's less orthodox researches.

Alongside his scientific advances, Newton had also made astonishing advances in his biblical studies. Whilst reading the earliest versions of the New Testament in their original languages he had become convinced that these texts had been corrupted by later translators and commentators for their own purposes. The idea of the Trinity (Father, Son and Holy Ghost) was a complete hoax, a fraudulent conception foisted on

Christianity by scheming deviants. Christ had not been divine, and we should pray directly to God the Father.

Such beliefs had been declared heretical by the Council of Nicea in 325AD. Likewise, the authorities of Trinity would not have welcomed the news that their college was named after a theological hoax – but this did not deter Newton. However, in keeping with his usual practice, he confined his findings to his notebooks.

In this case there was a need for Newton's secretive behaviour. Religion was taken very seriously indeed in 17th century England – the Civil War, the persecution of heretics, fear of Catholicism, distaste for Puritanism, and more, had produced a dangerous cocktail of prejudices. Not surprisingly, Newton developed a paranoid fear of being exposed as a heretic, and this was to last until the end of his days. But his profound belief in God, coupled with his unconscious need to communicate with Father directly, meant that he couldn't stop himself. Newton's impulse towards truth was as strong in religion as it was in science: here too he was searching for God's clues.

As if all this wasn't enough, Newton also continued with his alchemical researches in the hermetic tradition. The Lucasian Professor of Mathematics even went so far as to have a furnace constructed in the garden outside his college rooms, so that he could carry out alchemical experiments. His activities here were presumably passed off to the college authorities as chemistry, but one glance at Newton's notebooks makes it clear that his interest was in transmuting base metals into gold.

Incredibly, the first scientist of his age was also one of its leading sorcerers. As the 20th century economist Keynes pointed out: far from being a modern man of the new scientific era, Newton was in fact the last of the great Renaissance magicians 'the last wonder-child to whom the Magi could do sincere and appropriate homage'.

But was Newton really just wasting his time (and his prodigious talents) on balderdash? Concurring with sane opinion, Keynes found himself forced to dismiss Newton's alchemy as 'wholly devoid of scientific value'.

Alas, the truth is otherwise. Though it is unlikely that the Magic Circle will produce the next Einstein, there is no denying that alchemy played a central role in shaping Newton's *scientific* ideas. The evidence is unfortunately compelling. As we have seen, earlier in the century Descartes had proposed a purely mechanical explanation of the world. But as the scientific revolution progressed, a number of the new British scientists had begun to suspect that the world worked in a more complex fashion than the interior of a watch. In the view of the chemist Boyle (who was also an avid alchemist on the quiet) mechanics was not adequate to explain several natural phenomena occurring in chemistry and biology.

Newton conceived of the idea that such events were the result of an active principle, which complemented Descartes' mechanical inertia principle. This active principle was due to 'occult qualities . . . incapable of being discovered and made manifest'. From here it was but a short step to the notion of 'force', Newton's idea which was to transform the whole of science. It may be difficult for us to swallow, but the central revolutionary concept of Newton's Laws of Motion originated in magic. As that other great Renaissance magi Leonardo observed: 'There is more in the world than ever man will understand'.

Newton's alchemical activities also assisted him in other ways. Alchemy may have lacked demonstrable results (ie, no gold), but its methods involved considerable ingenuity – not least in the assembly of apparatus. (Much of this experimental expertise was adopted piecemeal by the embryo science of chemistry, which as a result got off to a flying start.) Newton had displayed exceptional practical expertise during his youth in Grantham, yet he had found less occasion for using this talent during his scientific and mathematical researches at Cambridge and Woolsthorpe. But for alchemy, he might even have avoided complex experimental endeavours. As it was, alchemy refined his practical abilities, which gave him confidence to seek practical solutions. The best-known example of this is his telescope.

As we have seen, when light passes through a prism it produces a spectrum. A similar side-effect takes place with lenses, which are liable to produce images with coloured fringes. This was beginning to hamper the effectiveness of the increasingly large telescopes being used in astronomy (the nuclear physics of the 16th-17th centuries, which opened up the new scientific era). By the turn of the 17th century, telescopes over 200 feet high were being built, but their magnified images were more and more subject to colour interference, known as 'chromatic aberration'. It looked as if telescopes had reached their limit, bringing an end to further astronomical discovery.

Newton first attempted to solve this problem by grinding different shaped lenses, but this proved unsuccessful. Once again he concentrated his mind on the problems involved: 'always thinking unto them', both night and day, until eventually he saw the answer. Newton's solution to the telescope problem was a classic 'stroke of genius'. It was so simple and effective that it transformed telescopes for ever. Instead of concentrating the final image by refraction through a lens, he did this with a parabolic mirror.

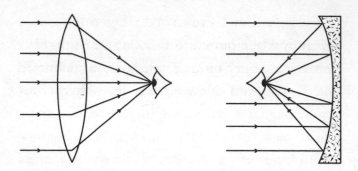

Reflection eliminated 'chromatic aberration' as the light did not pass through the glass, it merely bounced off it. And there was a further advantage to this method: as the light didn't pass through glass, none of it was absorbed. (This was vital in the observation of smaller distant bodies, such as the moons of Jupiter, which only reflected small amounts of light.) Newton's method also made the telescope much smaller. The first telescope which he produced was just six inches long and one inch in diameter – yet it had a magnification of over 30 times. Newton built this telescope entirely by himself, even going so far as to construct his own tools for the manufacture of certain parts. And to this day the most powerful telescopes continue to use reflecting dishes according to Newton's principle.

As Lucasian Professor of Mathematics, Newton was required to deliver a small number of lectures every term. These were ill-delivered and ill-prepared. Newton was no public communicator, and was more interested in talking about his continuing researches than in final results. After the initial clarity and excitement of the prism demonstration showing how white light is composed of colour, a fog of abstruse speculation and theory descended. In the end, Newton was often left muttering to himself in an empty lecture hall.

But this all changed when he produced his new telescope in 1668. Newton was so proud of his handiwork that for once he couldn't resist showing it off. Word began to spread through Cambridge, and eventually leaked out further afield. The Royal Society in London heard tell of this 'wondrous Instrument' and asked to see it. By now Newton was building a second larger version, which was nine inches long by two inches in diameter. In 1671 Barrow took this to London for him, where it caused such a sensation that it was demonstrated to Charles II. As a result, Newton was elected a member of the Royal

Society (which had been founded in 1660, and was now the leading scientific society in Europe). Newton at last had contact with the finest minds in the British scientific revolution.

Encouraged by this honour, Newton was persuaded to divulge some of his secrets. In 1672 he sent the Royal Society a paper on optics, describing his theory of light and colour. In the words of the secretary of the Royal Society, this paper 'mett both with a singular attention and an uncommon applause', though a few members demurred. Amongst these was the cantankerous physicist Hooke, one of the few scientists of sufficient calibre to contradict Newton. Hooke was an experimenter of genius, but seldom carried his insights through to fruition. He proposed an early, but ill-developed wave theory of light; he anticipated the steam engine, but in an impractical form; and his pioneering microscopic observations led him to invent the term 'cell' (though he applied it wrongly). Hooke had also undertaken experiments on light, using prisms, and had come up with a characteristically cock-eyed theory of his own. Hooke was a leading power at the Royal Society, and he considered optics to be his territory. He wrote a patronising critique of Newton's paper pooh-poohing his conclusions. Letters were exchanged, and when Newton published a second paper elaborating his findings Hooke accused him of plagiarism.

Newton was psychologically incapable of accepting criticism at the best of times. As a result of Hooke's accusation he was unable to contain himself, and his rage knew no bounds. Hooke became his sworn enemy – a role which the irascible Hooke was only too pleased to assume. But this was no passing fury on Newton's behalf. He was so upset by this incident that his work suffered for over two years. He acrimoniously resigned from the Royal Society (an unheard-of act, which fortunately was not accepted), and he swore that he would publish no further scientific work.

But still the controversy dragged on. Newton became involved in correspondence with some English Jesuits in Liège, who sought clarification of his original prism experiment. Their experiments had not produced the same effect which Newton claimed. This correspondence was to drag on for some years, with the Jesuits eventually denying the veracity of Newton's results. Already considerably agitated by this correspondence, Newton now mistook stupidity for conspiracy. His paroxysm became so great that he swore to abandon science: 'I will resolutely bid adew to it eternally' – and suffered a complete nervous breakdown.

While he recovered, Newton was as good as his word. He abandoned his scientific researches and buried himself in biblical and hermetic studies. To wit: the entire notion of the Trinity was rigged, only supported by fourth century documents forged by St Athanasius. Using the star regulus and copper it was possible magically to produce the hermaphrodite known as the net, which consisted of the male seed of Mars and the female principle of Venus. And so forth. (Newton's library consisted of over 140 books on alchemy alone; and according to a biographer, at his death his papers contained 'half a million worthless words on chemistry'.)

Then in 1679 Newton's mother died. He had been deserted by her for the last time: he was alone. It was Freud who first noted that the greatest intellectual insights often come to their discoverers after they have suffered a profound loss. And this was to be no exception. As a result of his occult notions concerning attraction and repulsion, Newton had conceived of the idea of forces. But so far he had only applied this notion to earth-bound phenomena. He now received a letter from Hooke, who wanted to patch up their differences. Hooke informed Newton about his analysis of planetary motion, including his idea of a central attraction which kept the planets in elliptical orbits. Hooke had guessed that this probably worked according to an inverse square law – unaware that Newton had worked out the mathematics of an inverse square law a decade or so previously.

Newton refused to be drawn into a lengthy correspondence with Hooke, but later admitted that Hooke's letter prompted him to apply his own inverse square law – whose mathematics was firmly based on Kepler's third law – to the elliptical orbits of the planets. It was this which in turn prompted Newton to one of his greatest insights. His notion of force – so far seen only in terms of terrestrial phenomena – also applied to orbital mechanics.

Newton was now on the brink of the concept of universal gravitation. But it was to be five years before the penny dropped. And once again this was prompted by his old *bête noire* Hooke.

In 1684 the odious Hooke bragged to the astronomer Halley that there was no longer any problem over planetary motion. He himself had worked out an inverse square law which governed the motion of heavenly bodies. Halley remained unconvinced by Hooke's explanation, which had little mathematical backing.

Halley decided to consult Newton, who informed him that he had produced a theory of orbital dynamics some years previously, and had the calculations to back it up. Halley managed to persuade Newton to send him a paper outlining his findings. Newton duly began a paper entitled 'On the Motion of Heavenly Bodies in Orbit' (*De motu corporum in gyrum*), which Halley received seven months later.

Halley was so impressed by this paper that he travelled once more to Cambridge, where he discovered that Newton had a vast store of unpublished papers. Halley's father had recently been murdered, leaving him a fortune. Halley suggested that he would be willing to finance the publication of Newton's papers.

Meanwhile the writing of *De Motu* had caused Newton to think beyond his ideas of planetary motion, and he had finally conceived of the idea of universal gravitation. In the flush of inspiration he agreed to Halley's scheme, and settled down to the necessary calculations.

For two and a half years Newton worked in isolation, producing the work which was to be his masterpiece: *Philosophiae naturalis principia mathematica* ('The Mathematical Principles of Natural Philosophy'). Nowadays this book, generally acknowledged as the finest work of science ever produced, is usually referred to simply as the *Principia*.

In keeping with the medieval custom which still prevailed, the *Principia* was written in latin (which continued to serve as the international language). Its full title stems from the fact that in those days science was still considered a branch of philosophy, and referred to as natural philosophy – though the implications of Newton's revolutionary work were to extend into philosophy itself. From now on, no philosopher could ignore this new cosmology, based upon experiment. It was no longer possible to explain the world by simply thinking about it and producing abstract principles. Concrete experience had to be taken into account. Heavily influenced by Newton's *scientific* discoveries, the philosopher Locke was to produce Empiricism, which states that our knowledge derives fundamentally from experience, thus laying the foundations of modern philosophy. Newton's *Principia* was to transform the entire way we thought about the world.

This work was also seen as one of the seminal works of the Age of Reason. An atmosphere of intellectual optimism began to prevail, science had shown that the world was constructed according to basic principles which could be elaborated according to reason. All could be known: science held the key to life, the universe and everything.

Yet paradoxically this most modern of books was not only written in latin, but set out in the style of the ancient Greeks. Its three laws of motion and Law of Universal Gravitation may have been the cornerstones of modern science,

but these were set down and proved by geo-
metrical reasoning, just as Euclid had done two
thousand years previously. Newton was aware
that he was writing a classic, and he wanted it to
be in the classic style. It would have been much
easier (and made much more sense) for him to
have used his new discovery, calculus. But this
new method, which would one day transform
mathematics, he preferred to keep a secret.
(There is only a passing reference to it in the
Principia; but as we shall see, this was to establish
a vital precedent.)

The manuscript of the *Principia* was first sent to
the Royal Society, whose secretary was now
Hooke. As soon as Hooke read Newton's manuscript, he accused Newton of plagiarism. He had
written to Newton six years previously divulging
his inverse square law. Newton had based his
work on stolen property.

The effect of this accusation was predictable.
Newton was unable to contain his rage. He had
discovered the inverse square law, and worked
out its mathematics, ten years before Hooke's
letter. But the trouble was, Newton had kept his
discovery to himself. Halley appealed to

Newton's better nature. Hooke was ill and ageing, his anti-social behaviour having reduced him to penury. All Hooke really required was some kind of acknowledgement – it would cost Newton nothing to make such a gesture in his *Principia*.

But Halley had underestimated Newton. He had no better nature – and his anger knew no bounds. Instead of inserting an acknowledgement into his work, Newton now vindictively searched through it eradicating all reference he could find to Hooke – though in the heat of the moment he did manage to miss a few. (Newton's fury was to be no passing matter. As long as Hooke remained secretary of the Royal Society, Newton refused to accept any post in it, refused to let it publish his works, and kept all his manuscripts to himself. Hooke was to linger on for 17 years, and this state of affairs was only resolved by his death in 1703.)

When Newton's *Principia* was finally published in 1687 it caused a sensation. Newton became internationally famous. Though his concept of 'force' was not generally accepted on the Continent, the leading scientists of the day soon recognised him as a worthy successor to Galileo and Descartes.

Meanwhile James II had introduced a campaign to transform Cambridge into a stronghold of Catholic learning. The academic staff resisted, and the author of the *Principia* became their unlikely champion. Newton, the covert heretic, at last had a legitimate target on which to vent his anxieties. His determined resistance to the king appeared brave and even reckless, though it was driven by forces which none suspected. Indeed, but for the flight of James II and the installation of a Protestant monarchy in the form of William and Mary, Newton would have found himself in extreme peril. Many went to the gallows for less.

In recognition of his stand, Newton was appointed a Member of Parliament for the University (which returned three unelected candidates at this period). Being an MP involved periods of residence in London. Here Newton found himself regarded with some awe, and was even invited to dine with the king. He was acknowledged as 'the finest of all thinkers' by Locke, whose acquaintance he made − along with such worthies as Wren (who was at the time completing St Paul's Cathedral), Pepys (the diarist and naval administrator, who had incongruously become president of the Royal Society) and Charles Montague (the ambitious politician who later became Lord Halifax). He also attracted a wide following amongst the younger generation of scientists, using his growing influence to have several of these appointed to the few paid university posts open to 'natural philosophers'.

Amongst these acolytes was one Fatio de Duillier, a young Swiss mathematician who had met the German philosopher-mathematician Leibniz and the Dutch physicist Huygens (inventor of the first genuinely accurate chronometer). Newton took an immediate liking to Fatio, and had soon formed a close emotional attachment to him. Generous references to Fatio even began appearing in Newton's scientific papers, acknowledging snippets of information which Fatio had passed on to him (a rare honour indeed). Newton took lodgings close to Fatio whilst in London, and Fatio even suggested that he should abandon living in Cambridge altogether and take up a post in London. According to Richard S. Westfall, Newton's great modern biographer, his relationship with Fatio 'was the most profound experience of his adult life'. When separated, they exchanged increasingly intense letters.

Falling in love (even if Newton remained unaware that this was what had happened to him), gave the 48-year-old scientist renewed energies. Besides genuine scientific work in optics, he flung himself into his alchemical pursuits with renewed enthusiasm. According to his assistant, he continued 'about 6 weeks in his Elaboratory (sic), the Fire scarcely going out either Night or Day, he sitting up one Night, as I did another, till he had finished his Chymical Experiments'. At the same time his increasing self-confidence emboldened him to write a paper explaining his religious 'findings'. He even showed this to Locke, who agreed to have it published anonymously in Holland. But at the last moment Newton got cold feet: disproving the Trinity might blacken the name of his college (let alone his name within it).

According to a legendary story, Newton almost blackened more than the name of his college. After working through the night, he set off one morning for church, absent-mindedly leaving a candle still burning on his desk. During his absence, this was knocked over by his dog Diamond. In the ensuing conflagration years of Newton's priceless unpublished work went up in flames. Upon returning from church, Newton is said to have exclaimed: 'Oh, Diamond! Diamond! Thou little knowest the mischief thou hast done'.

The pressure on Newton's already over-taxed mind became increasingly harmful. Towards the end of 1692 Newton appears to have undergone a crisis of faith in alchemy, which affected him deeply. At the same time another crisis was unfolding. Fatio had been seriously ill. Then suddenly he announced that his mother had died and he would have to return to Switzerland. Newton was distraught, despatching anguished letters to Fatio, begging him to move to Cambridge with him. Fatio prevaricated, deeply drawn to Newton. The exchange of letters reached fever pitch. And then suddenly stopped. We can only guess why.

Around this time, a fellow don noted that Newton suffered from 'a distemper that much seized his head, and left him awake for about five nights altogether'. The next four months are shrouded in silence. This is broken by a letter to Pepys, in which Newton informed him: 'I am extremely troubled at the embroilment I am in . . . nor have my former consistency of mind'. Three days later Locke received a scrawled ink-blotched letter from Newton, written at the Bull Tavern in Shoreditch, east London. In this he begs Locke's forgiveness for 'being of the opinion that you endeavoured to embroil me with woemen [and saying] 'twere better if you were dead'.

Newton had suffered another mental collapse, from which it took him nearly two years to recover. (Fatio seemingly suffered from an even worse breakdown, disappeared from the mathe-matical scene altogether, and was next heard of living with an extremist religious sect of French exiles.)

Newton was never again to undertake major scientific work – though he did produce sum-maries of previously unpublished work, which contributed considerably to his reputation. When Newton had recovered from his illness, his friends encouraged him to seek some prestigious post in London. (He obdurately refused the presidency of the Royal Society while Hooke was still hanging on as secretary.) Newton approached his political pal Montague, and was appointed Warden of the Mint, at the vast salary of £2,000 (at the time a skilled labourer was lucky to earn £20 a year).

The appointment of Newton to the Mint was intended as a well-earned sinecure: a reward for England's noblest intellectual ornament. Or so the official story goes. But according to his French admirer Voltaire: 'I supposed that the Court and the city of London named him Master of the Mint by acclamation. No such thing. Isaac Newton had a very charming niece who made a conquest of the minister Halifax Montague. Fluxions and gravitation would have been of no use without a pretty niece'. And curiously, it appears there may well have been some truth in this unlikely story.

Either way, Newton was not minded to regard his job as a sinecure. He had other ideas. At the time the English currency was being heavily undermined by forgers and 'clippers' (who snipped the edges off gold and silver coins). Once again, Newton had a legitimate target on which to vent his vast, suppressed rage. This time there was no danger (for him), and there was no stopping him. Within months Newton had become the terror of the London underworld, conducting a vindictive campaign against all the counterfeiters he could find. Over a hundred were flung into Newgate Jail, and Newton was responsible for a score of hangings at Tyburn. He insisted upon being present at all the trials.

Soon hardened criminals were literally trembling at the very mention of his name. Newton was out of control, touring the taverns (with an armed escort), conducting 'interviews' with suspects and informers. During the course of these 'interviews' he would give full vent to his fearsome rage – on hardened criminals and innocent alike. It was said that transcriptions of these interrogations, which presented only a formal version of the proceedings, read like the *Beggar's Opera*. Unfortunately Newton later destroyed these records – 'of whch wee burnt boxfuls,' according to the officer of the Mint who was his accomplice.

Newton's work soon began attracting attention beyond the confines of the underworld. A wealthy gentleman from Kensington called William Chaloner mounted a campaign against the Mint, accusing it of malpractice. He was known as an inventor, and suggested to parliament that the Mint's coining machines should be replaced with an invention of his own. Ever averse to disclosing his methods of work, Newton refused point blank to let Chaloner examine the Mint's coining machines. Whereupon Chaloner accused the Mint of making counterfeit coins, and being in league with the forgers.

This was a mistake. Newton had a lot to hide (heresy, etc), and was paranoid about accusations of secret malpractice. Newton 'investigated' Chaloner with merciless persistence, discovering from underworld informers that he had in fact made his fortune from counterfeiting coins. Although Chaloner had the protection of powerful friends, including well-placed MPs, Newton persisted with relentless passion. Chaloner was a ruthless man, betraying close colleagues who were sent to the gallows and issuing covert threats to Newton, in an attempt to elude justice. But Chaloner had called Newton a liar (which of course he was, every time he prayed in church). Newton could never rest while such a man lived. The result was inevitable. Chaloner was hung at Tyburn in 1699.

That same year, Newton was promoted to Master of the Mint, his salary increased to £3,500. By now Newton had been forced to transfer his attentions to more serious matters. Already clipping had reduced the entire silver coinage to almost half its specified weight, and as a result English money was frequently refused on the Continent. This was playing havoc with trade, and the Treasury was on the point of collapse. If this happened, the Protestant monarchy was liable to follow suit, with a recall of the dreaded Catholic Stuarts.

In desperation, the government decided there was only one solution: the entire currency would have to be recoined. Newton applied himself to this herculean task with characteristic single-mindedness. At the Mint 300 men and 50 horses (for turning the presses) were set to work, and £6,500,000 of currency was recoined in three years. This was some achievement: only half this amount had been produced in the previous 30 years!

In 1703 Hooke finally died, and Newton accepted the post of President of the Royal Society. Newton was incapable of magnanimity, and immediately ordered the burning of Hooke's portrait. He then set about revitalizing the Society, which had declined into a mere gossip shop. He instituted weekly meetings, at each of which a new experiment was demonstrated. Unlike previous presidents, who seldom turned up, Newton was only to miss three meetings in the next 20 years.

Newton's presidency was marred by further characteristic behaviour – only this time the victims were members of the Royal Society rather than the underworld. The most disgraceful episode concerned Flamsteed, the Astronomer Royal, whom Newton virtually hounded to his death.

Newton had crossed swords with Flamsteed whilst he was writing the *Principia*. In need of observational figures to support his calculations of the lunar orbit, Newton had written to

Flamsteed at the Royal Observatory in Greenwich. Flamsteed was a perfectionist, and had already spent over a decade making observations for what was to prove the most accurate and comprehensive map of the heavens yet undertaken. Newton required accurate figures immediately. Flamsteed was averse to letting the results of his long labours appear piecemeal; and only released the figures reluctantly, if at all. As a result, Flamsteed too eventually suffered Hooke's fate − all the acknowledgements to Flamsteed which Newton could find were vindictively erased from the second edition of the *Principia*. But this was just for starters.

When Newton became President of the Royal Society, the Royal Observatory effectively fell within his domain. He immediately ordered Flamsteed to publish all his findings forthwith. Flamsteed protested, and for many years fought a canny rearguard action against Newton's persistent bullying. But Newton was not easily thwarted. Eventually he inveigled his friend Halley into seizing Flamsteed's papers, his life's work. Halley was ordered to edit them himself for publication, and 400 copies appeared. Flamsteed was outraged, as well he might have been, at this desecration of his precious work.

He managed to obtain an injunction against the Royal Society, which was publishing the work. But too late, copies had already been distributed. With the aid of friends he managed to track down 300 copies, which he personally burnt. The Royal Society may have been the major institution of its kind in Europe, but its proceedings – especially those of its president – were sometimes far from scientific.

Now that Hooke was dead, Newton decided it was safe to publish more of his own work. (By this time no one in England had the temerity to question Newton, let alone accuse him of plagiarism.) In 1704 Newton published his second masterpiece, the *Opticks*. This was in fact little more than a summary of the groundbreaking work on light which he had done 30 years previously. Appended to this work were two papers outlining his method of fluxions (calculus), which he had also discovered some 30 years previously. Unfortunately the German philosopher Leibniz had published his own version of calculus 20 years previously. The inevitable accusations of plagiarism soon mounted to a furore.

The facts, such as we know them, are as follows. Leibniz had certainly seen some early papers of Newton's, but he had equally certainly worked out his own version of calculus independently. Indeed, his entire notation is different. (Leibniz's notation – such as $\int$ for integration – is the one we use today, as is his name for his discovery: calculus.) Newton's unwillingness to face questioning over his work condemned his fluxions to history. Leibniz's calculus was already being used by mathematicians on the Continent. Yet there's no doubt that Newton was the first to discover this method.

However, it soon became evident that the facts were of little concern to either side. (This sadly unscientific approach to priority disputes amongst scientists was quickly to become established as a tradition, which continues to flourish.) This time Newton had encountered an adversary even greater than Hooke – with an intellectual stature approaching his own, and an obduracy to match.

Leibniz made the tactical error of accusing

Newton of dishonesty, and once again Newton's anger knew no bounds. He became literally ill with rage. An acrimonious correspondence between members of the rival factions ensued, in the course of which the two greatest minds in Europe exhibited breathtaking unscrupulousness.

It was decided that the Royal Society should set up a committee to investigate the matter. Newton hijacked the committee's report, completely rewrote it in his own favour, and even anonymously reviewed it himself. He wrote numerous vituperative articles in his own favour, which he browbeat other eminent scientists and mathematicians into publishing under their own names. Leibniz did his own nasty best, and the controversy roared on until he died in 1714.

But Newton's rage was not so easily appeased. He continued to pursue Leibniz beyond the grave. Visitors spoke of spontaneous tirades against the dead German philosopher, and practically every scientific paper Newton wrote from then on included a furious paragraph castigating his deceased adversary. Leibniz was now unable to withdraw his accusation of dishonesty: so the stigma remained.

With justification, psychiatrists have speculated upon whether perhaps there was some deeper dishonesty in Newton's nature that he felt compelled to conceal. Was there something beyond all the heresy, the pathological anxieties that drove him to work day and night, the inability to tolerate questioning or accusations of any kind? Perhaps. It's possible that he was terrified by intimations of suppressed homosexuality, or some other secret he couldn't face. Yet if so, his flight from this truth of his own nature drove him to discover far more profound truths about nature itself. His failure as a human being – both psychologically and in his actions – would seem to have been inextricably bound up with his success in his work.

The tendency has been to see Newton's later years as the waste of a great talent. True, he produced nothing – but what could he have produced? Such questions are usually otiose. Yet in Newton's case there was certainly unfinished business. Take his views on light, for instance. Against the emerging opinion, Newton clung to the ancient view that light consisted of a stream of particles. Yet he was willing to concede that certain evidence appeared to confirm the opposing wave theory. Had he continued to put his mind to this problem, it's not impossible that he would have arrived at something resembling the quantum theory of light, which views it both as particles *and* waves. (It was to be 200 years before the Danish physicist Bohr developed this theory, thus instigating 20th century physics.)

Newton's supreme genius certainly waned after he arrived in London at the age of 43, but he remained nonetheless a match for any mind in Europe. In 1696 Leibniz had conceived of a problem, with the aid of his friend the Swiss mathematician Johann Bernoulli (who had helped Leibniz develop his version of integral calculus). The problem was as follows. Two points are selected at random on a vertical plane. What curve does a point follow when passing without friction under the force of gravity from the upper point to the lower point in the shortest time? This *Brachistochrone* (shortest time) problem was issued as a challenge to the leading minds of Europe. Newton received the details when he returned from work one afternoon after a hard day at the Mint. He was still averse to producing (or even discussing) his intellectual work in public, writing to a colleague: 'I do not love . . . to be dunned & teezed by forreigners about Mathematical things'. Despite this, he couldn't resist casting his eye over the problem after dinner, and by four in the morning he had solved it. The curve is a cycloid, the trace left by a point on the circumference of a circle as it rolls along a straight line. Next day Newton despatched his solution anonymously; but Bernoulli knew at once who was responsible, making his celebrated remark: 'I recognise the lion by his claw'.

Twenty years later, when Newton was 74, Leibniz decided to have another dig at his old enemy – issuing a problem which he pretended was a challenge 'to the brotherhood of fine mathematical enquirers'. (In modern parlance this asked: for any one-parameter family of curves, what are the orthogonal trajectories?) This question concealed a devious trap. Once again, Newton received the problem when he returned from work at the Mint, and had solved it before he went to bed, circumventing the brilliant trap as an irrelevancy. Leibniz refrained from comment; no further challenges were issued, and a year later he was dead.

Newton's hair had turned grey when he was in his early thirties – 'a Metamorphosis occasion'd by extremity of Concentration upon his Studies', according to a fellow don. But physically he was to remain in excellent health to the end of his days. He never needed glasses and he only ever lost one tooth. Contemporary sources claim that he lived frugally, even meanly. (French visitors to his home complained of 'inedible fare, with paucity and poorness of the vintage in equal degree'. But then the French always made such remarks when visiting England.) However, Newton's diet appears to have been frugal only by 18th century standards. A typical weekly bill for household items includes a goose and a chicken, two turkeys and two rabbits; and when he died he owed no less than £7 and ten shillings to his brewer (itemised as *fifteen* barrels of beer.) Such hardly speaks of saintly abstinence.

Newton remained Master of the Mint until the end of his life. He was also re-elected annually to the presidency of the Royal Society (none dared oppose him). Even in his eighties he dutifully attended the weekly meetings, only occasionally dozing off during the proceedings. He also prepared later editions of his *Principia* and the *Opticks*, and continued avidly with his theological speculations, producing such works as *Upon the Prophecies of Daniel and the Apocalypse of St John* and the *Chronology of the Ancient Kingdoms Amended* (in which he calculated the exact date when the world had begun, according to his own interpretation of the biblical texts). He always found something to occupy him. And according to his psychological biographer Manuel: 'Busyness, that false balsam of anxiety, took the form of obsessively copying when there was nothing else to do'.

During his last years Newton was looked after by his niece – no longer a London beauty – and her husband, who conscientiously noted down the great old man's stories and memories. Isaac Newton, the finest scientist who ever lived, finally died on March 20th 1727, at the age of 84.

He was buried in pomp at Westminster Abbey, his pall supported by dukes, earls and the Lord Chancellor, his funeral attracting vast crowds.

Voltaire, who was visiting London at the time, marvelled: 'England honours a mathematician as other nations honour a king who has done well by his subjects'.

SOME QUOTES

The rejected epitaph for Newton's tomb:

'Nature, and nature's laws lay hid in night.
God said, *Let Newton be!* and all was light.'

Alexander Pope.

Lines said to have been written on seeing Newton's statue in the chapel at Trinity College by moonlight:

'. . . Newton, with his prism, and silent face:
The marble index of a mind for ever
Voyaging through strange seas of Thought,
alone.'

The Prelude, William Wordsworth

Einstein's introduction to a new edition of the *Opticks*:

'Fortunate Newton, happy childhood of science!

. . . Nature to him was an open book, whose letters he could read without effort. The conceptions which he used to reduce the material of experience to order seemed to flow spontaneously from experience itself, from the beautiful experiments which he ranged in order like playthings and describes with an affectionate wealth of detail . . . Newton's age has long since been passed through the sieve of oblivion, the doubtful striving and suffering of his generation has vanished from our ken; the works of some great thinkers and artists have remained, to delight and ennoble us and those who come after us. Newton's discoveries have passed into the stock of accepted knowledge.'

Newton's definition of force from the *Principia*:

'An impressed force is an action exerted upon a body, in order to change its state, either of rest, or of uniform motion in a right line.

This force consists in the action only, and remains no longer in the body when the action is over. For a body maintains every new state it acquires, by its inertia only. But impressed forces are of different origins, as from percussion, from pressure, from centripetal force.'

Leibniz's opinion of Sir Isaac Newton, before they fell out:

'Leibniz said that taking Mathematicks from the beginning of the world to the time of Sir I. what he had done was much the better half – & added that he had consulted all the learned in Europe upon some difficult point without having any satisfaction and that when he wrote to Sir I. he sent him answer by the first post to do so and so and then he would find it out.'

'Responsio': in reply to the Queen of Prussia

From Newton's account of planetary motion:

'Centripetal forces are directed to the individual centres of the planets.

That there are centripetal forces actually directed to the bodies of the sun, of the earth, and other planets, I thus infer.

The moon revolves about our earth, and by radii drawn to its centre describes areas nearly proportional to the times in which they are described, as is evident from its velocity compared with its apparent diameter; for its motion is slower when its diameter is less (and therefore its distance greater), and its motion is swifter when its diameter is greater.

The revolutions of the satellites of Jupiter about that planet are more regular; for they describe circles concentric with Jupiter by uniform motions, as exactly as our senses can perceive.

And so the satellites of Saturn are revolved about this planet with motions nearly circular and uniform, scarcely disturbed by any eccentricity hitherto observed.'

CHRONOLOGY OF NEWTON'S LIFE

1642   Born in hamlet of Woolsthorpe, Lincolnshire.

1644   His mother remarries and moves to nearby village, leaving Isaac to be brought up by his grandmother.

1653   Mother returns home after death of her second husband.

1659   Mother calls Isaac back from school in Grantham to look after the farm.

1661   Goes to Trinity College, Cambridge as a sizar.

1665   Receives BA from Cambridge and flees back home to Woolsthorpe to avoid the Plague.

1665–6 Newton's *annus mirabilis*, during which he receives the inspiration for his law of gravity.

1667   Returns to Cambridge, elected Fellow

of Trinity College.

1669   Becomes Lucasian Professor of
        Mathematics at Cambridge.

1672   Elected a Fellow of the Royal Society.

1678   Suffers first nervous breakdown after
        controversy with Hooke.

1687   Publishes *Principia Mathematica*.

1693   Suffers mental collapse after break with
        Fatio.

1696   Moves to London and becomes
        Warden of the Mint.

1699   Promoted to Master of the Mint.

1703   Accepts presidency of the Royal
        Society on the death of Hooke.

1704   Publishes *Opticks*.

1727   Dies at the age of 84.

Chronology of Era

1642   Death of Galileo.
        Outbreak of Civil War in England.
        Dutch explorer Tasman maps coast of
        Van Diemen's Land (now Tasmania).

1648   End of Thirty Years War leaving large
        tracts of Germany devastated.

1649   Execution of Charles I and proclamation

of the Commonwealth, the first successful revolution and establishment of a
republic in a major European country.

1650   Death of Descartes.

1660   End of the Commonwealth and
Restoration of Charles II to the throne.

1664–5 Plague spreads through England.

1665   Death of great French mathematician
Fermat.

1669   English government draws up
constitution for the colony of The
Carolinas in America.

1688   Glorious Revolution: James II flees the
country and the Protestant monarchs
William and Mary ascend to the throne.

1690   Locke publishes *An Essay Concerning
Human Understanding*, instigating
philosophy of Empricism.

1706   Act of Union between English and
Scottish parliaments establishes Great
Britain.

1715   Louis XIV the 'Sun King' dies at
Versailles.

1716   Death of German mathematician-
philosophcr Lcibniz.

SUGGESTIONS FOR FURTHER READING

Richard S. Westfall: *Never at Rest* (Cambridge 1996) – the definitive modern biography

John Fauvel (ed): *Let Newton Be* (Oxford 1995) – perspectives on his life and works

Frank E. Manuel: *A Portrait of Isaac Newton* (Cambridge 1968) – the best psychological study

Bernard Cohen (ed): *Newton* (London 1995) – texts, backgrounds and commentaries.

Ivars Peterson: *Newton's Clock* (London 1996) – Newton and beyond: Chaos in the Universe.